TIME MANAGEMENT
Made Easy

D0731614

TIME MANAGEMENT
Made Easy

Patty Marler ■ Jan Bailey Mattia

VGM Career Horizons
NTC/Contemporary Publishing Group

Library of Congress Cataloging-in-Publication Data

Marler, Patty.
    Time management made easy / Patty Marler, Jan Bailey Mattia.
       p.   cm.
    ISBN 0-8442-4324-8
    1. Time management.   I. Mattia, Jan Bailey.   II. Title.
HD69.T54M378   1998
640′.43—dc21   97-47712
                                                    CIP

Cover photograph copyright © Francisco Cruz/Superstock
Cover design by Amy Ng
Interior design by City Desktop Productions, Inc.

Published by VGM Career Horizons
A division of NTC/Contemporary Publishing Group, Inc.
4255 West Touhy Avenue, Lincolnwood (Chicago), Illinois 60646-1975 U.S.A.
Printed in the United States of America
International Standard Book Number: 0-8442-4324-8
18   17   16   15   14   13   12   11   10   9   8   7   6   5   4   3   2   1

To Justin, Bailey, and Jeff . . .

You are my number one priority.
May my life and the things I do always reflect my love for you.

—Patty Marler

Contents

Introduction

"Time management made easy" seems like a bit of a contradiction in terms because we all know how little time we have and how many things we're committed to. Well, no one said it would be *that* easy!

Although *Time Management Made Easy* offers no quick fixes, it will help you take a serious look at where your priorities are and where your time needs to be spent. If you are truly committed to managing yourself and making some changes in the speed your life is moving, then *Time Management Made Easy* is for you.

Prepare to do some soul-searching, realigning, and positive growing!

Let him that would move the world, first move himself.

Socrates

Special Features

Special features throughout the book will help you pick out key points and discover new things about yourself and others.

 Notes clarify text with concise explanations.

 Helpful Hints provide ideas and suggestions to improve your self-management skills.

 Reflecting Moments are thoughts to ponder to help identify your priorities and values.

 Life Bytes are stories of real people and how their time-management decisions affected their lives.

 Chaos Calibrators are gauges to help you evaluate whether or not you are spreading chaos around you.

 Special Thoughts provide inspiration and motivation.

Chapter 1

Changing Time?
Changing Times

Time goes, you say? Ah no!
Alas, Time stays, **we** go.

Austin Dobson

Perhaps this book is poorly named. Time management is really not all that easy when it comes right down to it; in fact, it's impossible! We cannot manage time; we can only manage ourselves.

By dictionary definition, time is a constant, a systematic passing of a specific duration. Why, then, does it seem time is speeding up? Speak with your parents or your grandparents, and consider your own life. As you age, does time pass you by more quickly than ever? Do you have less time to do the things you want? Do the days, weeks, and years slip by with ever increasing speed? How many times have you found yourself reminiscing about something in the past and then catching yourself with "Oh, my goodness, that was ten years ago"?

Why? We will assume the earth is still spinning at the same rate and time is ticking along at a constant. What, then, is happening to us as individuals and as a society that makes us certain that time is traveling faster?

Take a moment to reflect on the past year of your life and jot down what you feel are the important moments. Do they exist, or is the year simply a blur of daily tasks?

Granted, as we age and the responsibilities of adulthood creep into our lives, there are certainly more things to steal time in the day. As kids, time traveled *sooo* slowly. No deadlines, no appointments, no lunch meetings or errands to run, just days filled with whatever happened, wherever it happened. As we got older, there were more distractions—more stuff—but there has to be more to it than simply aging.

What?

Capitalizing on Convenience

In an age of convenience stores, fast cars, microwave ovens, high-speed commuter trains, cellular telephones, fax machines, and countless other efficiency-increasing devices, it seems ridiculous to speak of how little time we have to ourselves. How can we possibly have so many time-saving conveniences and so little time? Our childhood has definitely slipped away from us at breakneck speed!

It seems as the speed with which we *can* do things increases, we find ourselves wanting to do more, even faster. Think about your own time and the things you incorporate into your daily life. Can you remember how you ever survived without a cellular telephone in your car to keep in touch with your family or with the office, or to call ahead for pizza while you were on your way to get it?

One by one the sands are flowing,
One by one the moments fall;
Some are coming, some are going:
Do not strive to grasp them all.

Adelaide A. Proctor

Can you imagine how you ever did business without a fax machine? The mail is so painfully slow, how on earth did we manage to get urgent business done on time? Sure, there were overnight couriers, but how can that compare to the same-minute service of a fax?

Before answering machines and voice mail, my goodness, it's a wonder we ever kept in touch with friends and family. You know how it is: "Have your machine call my machine and we'll get together some day, real soon."

 **How often do you find yourself hoping for people's voice mail so you don't have to take the time to talk to them?**

Or the big one, life without a computer. We marvel at the thought of it when we hear there are people who still write letters by hand, compose university papers with pen and paper, or even sit at a typewriter to develop manuscripts for novels. Where do these people find the time in their days to sit for that long?

We are surrounded by *instant*. We, as a society, do not want things now—we want them yesterday! Consider the evolution of some of these conveniences:

- Fast-food restaurants weren't fast enough, so drive-through windows were added.

- Heaven forbid we had to stand in line at the bank, so automatic banking machines appeared.

- Now, it would be so much faster if we didn't actually have to get out of our cars to use the instant teller. Drive-through banking is born.

- Oh, wait, we're not done yet. Wouldn't it be great if we could do our banking without even having to get close to a bank? Telephone banking arrives.

- Buying eyeglasses used to take a day or two. Now you can have your prescription filled in about an hour.

- Your holiday photos were ready overnight, but that meant you couldn't look them over at dinner that evening. Now they are ready for you the same day.

- Retail stores were open 10–6 Monday to Friday. Then they opened Saturdays. That wasn't enough, so they chose some nights to stay open till 9. Now many stores are open Sunday, and some are open twenty-four hours a day.

Obviously this list could go on and on. We have convenience and speed, but that never seems to be quite enough. We want personalized service, on our terms, on our schedule, as fast as it can humanly (or mechanically) be done. From dry cleaning to flights around the world, the faster, the more frequent, the more convenient, the better. Argh! The jet-setting speed and stress of it all.

 **Think of the people in your life with a youthful spirit. What is there to learn about what keeps them young and less consumed by stress?**

Is this speed really necessary? Are we so busy we can't afford the time to leave our pants one extra day at the dry cleaners? Are we simply so disorganized that we forget about having them cleaned until we absolutely must have them, or have we become so accustomed to having things done the instant we want them that we don't bother to plan ahead before we are out of time and completely desperate?

 Things do not change; we change.

Henry David Thoreau

Perhaps we need to ask ourselves if all these time-saving devices have streamlined our lives and made us more efficient and productive; do they just keep us running consistently faster, or have they simply made us less responsible? We are all guilty at one time or another of leaving things to the absolute last minute, and there are obviously occasions when that will continue to happen. But if we knew we had to plan ahead, if we knew there wasn't a twenty-four-hour convenience store right around the corner, would we leave so many things to the last minute?

Aaron never bothered to maintain his vehicle; he simply had difficulty finding the time. It broke down on the way to the airport . . . he missed his flight.

We are what we repeatedly do. Excellence, then, is not an act, but a habit.

Aristotle

The next time you find yourself in a big rush to complete something, take a breath and ask yourself, "Is this really that important? Will the world stop turning if it's not done?"

Ripples of Time

Take a minute and refer to your own life. How many times a day do you find yourself the unwitting victim of someone else's time-management nightmare?

Consider these time-management disasters waiting to happen:

• Someone speeding to an appointment cuts you off in traffic.

- The waiter at lunch, thinking about an overdue university paper, forgets to deliver your order to the kitchen, and you are late getting back to the office.

- You have to wait in line longer at the post office because a woman rushed in, out of breath, desperately pleading to be served ahead of you because she was running late.

- Completion of your family portrait is delayed because the photographer bumped your order back to complete a rush anniversary photo a husband wanted done for his wife.

- Someone was generally rude to you because he or she was behind schedule and stressed, and you just happened to be there.

- You find the tempo and stress of your day increasing and the panic factor creeping in because someone close to you is operating in high gear and his or her chaotic energy rubs off.

 Spend a day taking note of how many times you are affected by someone else's lack of planning.

The ripple effect of poor time management, as you perhaps now are beginning to see, can be quite profound. Even if you work hard to be organized and maintain a healthy Zen approach to life, if you are surrounded by people making poor time-management choices, it is easy to find yourself unsuspectingly, and unwillingly, caught in their wake.

Be aware of how your life is affected by the way other people manage (or don't manage!) their lives. The people you work with, family, friends, and people you simply come in contact with on a casual basis all have the ability to affect you and the management of your life. Take the time to notice who in your life has the tendency to create chaos wherever they go. Who brings with them that harried feeling, that feeling that everything is urgent, that there is never enough time and, oh my goodness, how will we ever make it through this?

 Equally as important, how often are you the origin of chaos ripples that negatively affect those around you?

Certainly you can't go around choosing your friends and work associates solely on the basis of their time-management skills, but their habits are something you need to be aware of. As we allow time in society to continue to speed up and we push ourselves to do more and more in a day, it is becoming increasingly important to surround ourselves with those who can still maintain a healthy sense of perspective and calm amidst the chaos.

Dean's friend, Chris, was always "up," always on the go, constantly talking at high speed of what else needed to be done, and lamenting to Dean all the while about the overwhelming stress of it all—so much so that it was physically tiring for Dean to be around him. Dean quickly began to prefer to be with him when Chris was depressed, or a little down, because the constant frenzy of "gotta go, gotta do, gotta be" would calm down long enough so the two friends could actually talk.

Surround yourself with people who have a clear understanding of what is important to them. People who have clearly defined goals, a strong desire to create positive relationships with those around them and the strength to see through the chaos to what is truly important— these are the people to align yourself with and to learn from. Efficient time management is a life choice, a process of streamlining, an exercise in self-knowledge and discipline; no one mentioned it would be easy.

Don't **say** things. What you **are** stands over you the while, and thunders so that I cannot hear what you say to the contrary.

Ralph Waldo Emerson

Remember, time has not changed; it remains a constant, and it remains up to you how you wish to manage yourself within it.

The Umbilical Cord of Technology

In theory, with all the technology available to us, time management should be a breeze. We are never out of touch. From answering machines to pagers, voice mail, and cell phones, laptop computers to E-mail and car faxes, if people want to reach us for urgent business, casual conversation, or just plain curiosity of our whereabouts, they can, and they can do it instantly.

Consider your life. When you actually want people to get in touch with you, how many numbers do you give them? Cell phone? Pager? Voice mail? Fax? Message center? Office? Home? E-mail? How many numbers are there on your business card? Where in your world can you go to get away from the ringing, buzzing, and beeping of the technology that surrounds you? With satellite linkups and the Internet at our fingertips, the world is shrinking rapidly and, with it, so is our own personal space. What does this mean to you?

 Things which matter most must never be at the mercy of things which matter least.

Johann Wolfgang von Goethe

It means it is becoming increasingly difficult to achieve any type of division between what is your time and what is public time. There is a gray area now where, not long ago, there was a very clear distinction of private versus public. Think about the simple things:

- The phone. Not all that long ago if the phone rang in your home or your parents' home after 9:00 P.M., it must have been some sort of emergency.

- Sunday was a day for family activity, never work. That was simply the way it was.

- You were at the office from 9–5 and after that your time was your own. Your boss did not call you at home to discuss work. It could wait till tomorrow morning.

- You participated in one or two extracurricular activities, which took up two or three nights a week. The rest of your time was your own.

- The entire family sat down to dinner, together, every night.

Today, the rules are not so clear, and that gray area is expanding. What are the hours in your home when the phone never rings, even if just for a social call? Are there hours in your day when the people you work with and your friends know you are simply unavailable? Now, more than ever, because of how accessible we have become and how in-touch we constantly are, it is important to establish clear time boundaries. You must choose the times in your life when you are unavailable to outside calls and impositions and stick to that, without feeling guilty.

LB

Mohammed had a summer assignment to complete for graduate school in the fall. It seemed like he had forever to work on it, so he took his time starting. When he finally got around to it, he had numerous houseguests and a contract employment position he couldn't refuse, and he felt obligated to help two friends move apartments. Two days before the project was due Mohammed was starting it. He was forced to ask for an extension and lose marks.

Ultimately, we have no time to ourselves because we allow no time for ourselves. Somewhere along the evolutionary time line of society, we decided if people were not constantly busy and constantly in-touch, they were ineffective.

For many of us, our dependence on technology has become an unhealthy addiction. Addiction? Yes, addiction.

ST

People, for the sake of getting a living, forget to live.

Margaret Fuller

How can you tell if you are addicted to technology? There are some telltale signs to be aware of:

1. You still feel naked in the morning after you dress until your pager is clipped to your belt.

2. As you are driving a commercial comes on the radio with a cell phone sound effect ringing in the background. You get a little adrenaline rush and catch yourself reaching for your phone.

3. You find there is no room on your business card for your company logo because there is too much phone, fax, and E-mail information taking up space.

4. You find yourself in a movie theater wanting to make one last call on your cell phone while the previews are playing.

5. You are in the car, with a business associate, driving to play golf. You are talking on your cell phone. You look toward the passenger seat—she is on her cell phone as well.

6. You are having a romantic dinner with your spouse when somewhere in the restaurant a cell phone rings. You automatically reach for your phone before you realize the call isn't yours. You laugh, pause, and suddenly think of a call you could make. You pick up your cell phone and start to dial. Picture your spouse leaving the restaurant without you.

Okay, some of these are a little far-fetched . . . or are they? Sadly, some of them are not all that out there. We are calling technology convenient, but if we take a good look at it we might more appropriately call some of it overkill.

 Honestly think about it, how much negative impact would it have on your effectiveness as a human being if you disconnected yourself from your array of technology after 9:00 P.M.?

The world is full of cactus. But we don't have to sit on it.

Will Foley

There is no question that technical wizardry can be entertaining to experiment with, fun to have, convenient to use, and, occasionally, downright essential. The questions that do arise, however, are how much is enough and when does too much turn into silly? Obviously, when you have a cell phone and a pager and you check your voice mail religiously every half hour, there are some questions you may need to ask yourself.

What, in your life, is so important that you need to constantly check in, and are you sure it is that important? Work? Extracurricular activities? A jealous spouse? A busy social calendar? *What are you sacrificing for this constant staying in touch?* Personal space? Rejuvenation or downtime? Family? Friends? Quality, uninterrupted relationships? *Living?*

There are exceptions to every rule, of course. Sometimes real emergencies *do* arise. For example, if your brother is sick in the hospital, you want to be in touch and available at all times in case you are needed. By all means, use the technology as it was intended. If you've been called away from the office but an important document only you can sign is arriving some time today by courier, yes, you are genuinely needed for this one—turn on the cell phone. If you are a contract employee expecting a call from potential employers and you want to be accessible so they don't hire the next name on the list, go to it; plug in, wire up, do what you need to do to pay rent and feed the gerbil. If you're on the highway alone in freezing winter conditions complete with icy roads, it would seem silly to not have your cell phone with you!

However, if the only reason you can come up with for having every technological device known to man wired to your belt or to the lighter in your car is "Gee, someone might need to get in touch with me," perhaps you should do some re-evaluating.

For a week, keep a log of how many times your cell phone rings, your pager beeps, or you have E-mail at home. How many of those are essential, absolutely-could-not-wait-till-tomorrow messages?

Ask yourself honestly:

- What is it you do at home or at the office that makes you totally indispensable?

- Are you *really* indispensable?

- Why is it only you who can solve a particular problem or put out a particular fire?

- Have you bothered to train any of the people around you?

- Do you trust the people around you?

- Are the people around you unable or unwilling to take on responsibility because you've not taken the time to ensure that they had the confidence and ability to readily assume leadership roles when necessary?

- Do you enjoy being the one with a finger on the pulse of everything in your life, the one in control?

Before this turns into a lecture on ego downsizing, there is, in fact, a point. Today, work is a dominating force in everyone's life—work, or the lack of it, that is. As a result, there will be times when you will be called upon to take time from your personal life to perform work-related duties. This does not mean, however, you must become a slave to work and the accompanying technology, unable to set limits, or unable to trust anyone else with important responsibilities.

 Use the term work as it applies to you, whether you are a homemaker or an office executive.

We must be willing to share responsibilities. This means within families and at the office you must learn to decide what is important now and in the long term, and you must clearly share that vision with the people around you so everyone is working to the same end. Take the time now to invest in training and long-range planning that will leave you the time to focus on what is truly important in your life. Learn to trust that the people in your life at home and at work are capable people and it's okay to turn your pager off now and again. Chances are fairly good that if you miss a page or a call, the world will continue to turn.

Life in a Beer Commercial

One of the primary reasons people feel a lack of personal time is our perpetual quest to keep up with the Joneses. Every passing generation wants more materially for themselves and for their children. At what cost?

. . . I was taught that the way of progress is neither swift nor easy.

Marie Curie

What has become the standard by which we judge if we are indeed keeping up with those around us? How do we decide if we are happy, successful, and fulfilled? It seems that, rather than looking within ourselves for the answers to these most personal questions, we have resorted to comparing ourselves to friends, associates, and the people we see on TV.

We've succumbed to the mentality that "my life would be perfect if I lived in a beer commercial. If I could achieve that lifestyle, things would truly be perfect: great parties in the backyard, fabulous trips to the cabin with beautiful friends and neighbors, cool concerts in amazing locations, and never a dull moment. Undoubtedly I would drive a slick car, wear hip clothes, and never, never have a bad hair day!"

Just to keep it in perspective, remember—if the people in beer commercials actually drank as much beer as they seem to, they certainly wouldn't look like they do!

It gets worse. Our brain takes another step and we start to think, "Obviously, I must be doing something wrong in my life if I can't be like that. I must add more activities to my life in hope of finding that lifestyle, that ultimate peer group where all the coolness in the world culminates! If I work harder and longer, I can get there, be that." And life goes on, in a desperate quest to take up residence in a make-believe world.

Now is the time to say: *don't do that!* Don't compare yourself to something that doesn't exist; don't modify your life in an attempt to create it.

We are all guilty, at some point in each of our lives, of sitting and thinking, "I'd love to trade places with them." Where does this realization leave us? It leaves us at the beginning. We do not live in a beer commercial—no one does—and only we can define what it is that truly makes us happy. A continual race with time to keep up with the Joneses will not lead to a life of happiness and fulfillment: our lives, our happiness, our definition. Granted, it isn't an easy task to decide what you want out of life and to commit yourself to totally go for it, but when you consider the options . . .

 O, how bitter a thing it is to look into happiness through another man's eyes.

William Shakespeare

There is only so much time in a day. At the end of it all, you need to be happy with what you have done and with what you have become.

Children's Hours

Having reminisced briefly about our childhood and the seemingly endless days of summer, we need to look at how today's children are affected by society's frantic pursuit of the ultimate existence. Are we creating a generation of individuals totally unsatisfied unless they are constantly busy and continually stimulated by outside interests? Are our children losing their ability to play, to imagine, to simply be kids?

While we are so busy trying to make money and entertain our children, to find new and exciting experiences for them that we were not exposed to, while we whisk them off day after day to different places to do different activities and extracurricular events, perhaps we should stop and ask ourselves if we are, in fact, doing them a favor or a huge injustice. Have we taken away the innate nature of children to imagine and create what they would like to do with their days?

 Take a look at your weekly **family** planner. (If you don't have one, create one with your family.) How much time are you spending with your children? Where can you add more?

At a time when we are so anxious about our lack of time, we have assumed yet another responsibility we had no need to totally assume. Plan activities to stimulate the growth of your children, absolutely, but plan to give them time alone to imagine, to learn, and to decide for themselves what their days will hold. Encourage your children to take responsibility for designing their own activities. Invite them to plan an afternoon for the family—you may be surprised by what they consider an exciting, entertaining, or fulfilling day.

 Marguerite was busy organizing summer projects for her daughter and didn't find the time to play with her much. By the

time she realized it, it was too late. It took Marguerite's
daughter two weeks to get over being hurt and angry with her.

By all means be involved in what your children do, but remember
to let them plan their own time as well because it's truly amazing what
can unfold in an afternoon of watching the clouds drift by. It's
shocking, sometimes, what you can learn about yourself and your
children if you spend the day building a fort in the backyard. Instead
of so desperately trying to cram as many experiences into the lives of
our children as possible, perhaps we would do well to slow down for a
day or two, hang out in the yard with them, and see what there is to
be seen in the clouds. For their growth—and for ours.

o the Moon

The world is, in fact, shrinking. It seems as every day passes, technology gets faster and the world becomes smaller. We've been to the
moon, we've had robot messengers transmitting information to us
from Mars, and we have satellites sending us information from all over
the cosmos. We can E-mail a message anywhere in the world in a
matter of seconds, and we can invite anyone we wish into our homes
via the magic of videoconferencing.

Why do we do it? Because we can. It is human nature to strive to
grow, to learn, and to do. Why do we push ourselves to the limit of
our capacity, cramming more and more into each minute? Because we
can. Why do we speed from one appointment to another, constantly
changing hats along the way? Because we can. The world is so full of
experiences, people, and places, and we want to meet, see, and touch
all of them, because we can.

Somewhere along the time line of our social growth many of us
lost touch with the simplicity of life. Add to that what seems to be
an intrinsic need, whether we have children or not, to pass more than
we had along to the next generation. Somehow, in some way, we all

strive to make life better, easier, happier for our children and our children's children.

 LB

Kristen has been very busy with two big projects at work and hasn't taken any time for herself. The stress has accumulated in her neck and gives her such pain and headaches she's forced to squeeze massage therapy in every day before work.

So now what do you do?

You work harder, faster, longer, at breakneck speed, desperately trying to fit everyone and everything in and make enough money to enjoy it all. Well . . . no.

You do have to work harder—no, *smarter*—at defining your roles in life. Having decided that time is a constant, only you can manage yourself to create the kind of world you want to live in.

Ask yourself:

- What kind of person do I want to be?

- Who are the people I want and need in my life?

- Who and what do I want to be to them and for them?

- What am I willing to sacrifice to be with them?

- What kind of effect do their time-management ripples have on me?

- Remembering that I cannot change the behavior of other people, only my own, are the people in my life helping me become the person I want to be, or are they simply adding more confusion for me to sort through?

Chapter 2

Creating Chaos

You're not managing your time, so what? It's your life, your business, your time . . . you can do with it what you like. It's not really bothering you, and you're the only person affected, right?

Wrong!

Your disorganization and need for time management affects more people than you may believe. And it affects *you* more than you want to believe.

Time Management? Who Needs It?

Traditionally, time-management strategies have been geared toward corporate executives, ranging from to-do lists to day planners and goal-setting workshops. But is this really time management? Are quick fixes, gadgets, and seminars really the answer? Do only corporate executives need it? Let's take a look.

 LB

Brenda was a doer, the kind of person every committee and organization wanted. She had good ideas and the drive and determination to make them reality. She worked hard and in her wake left completed tasks, pleasing the most critical of employers.

After several years of successful employment, Brenda began a family and made the career decision to remain at home. She planned to focus her efforts on her children and do the same

19

kind of job as a mother that she had done with all her previous endeavors. She was going to be a successful parent.

Brenda directed considerable time and effort to her first child and still found some time to spare. She began volunteering and put the same effort into volunteering that she put into all her endeavors. One project well done led to another and, within a few years, Brenda was known at several different organizations as someone with the energy and commitment to be of great benefit.

As a result, more requests were made for Brenda's time, and the little projects became bigger. She found she was a spouse, the parent of two active children, the coordinator for a large Sunday school program, planning and leading monthly parenting support meetings for an international organization (as well as completing all the required documentation and peripheral tasks associated with the organization), offering parenting workshops, writing monthly articles for a local newspaper, and doing some freelance work at home to keep her in touch with her previous profession. What a woman!

Suddenly, Brenda no longer looked for things to fill her time; she looked for time to fulfill her commitments. Plus, Brenda still could not settle for anything less than very well done (she did decide perfection was unrealistic, but less than superb was unacceptable). Time management undoubtedly became an issue.

Brenda's example illustrates several points.

First, although time-management literature and workshops often target white-collar employees, time-management skills are for everyone: blue-collar workers, students, stay-at-home parents, volunteers, and, yes, company executives—people from all walks of life. Your position title does not determine whether or not you need time-management skills. How you live your life determines whether or not you need to work on managing your time.

 **Needing to evaluate your time management does not mean you are disorganized or lazy. On the contrary, often well-organized, meticulous perfectionists take on too much and discover time is a problem. What sort of person are you?**

Second, quick fixes aren't the answer. No matter how many electronic organizers, day planners, and to-do lists Brenda made, her life would still be a time-management disaster. There comes a time you simply must cut back on your activities. Simple answer, not so easy to do.

Third, the need for managing time is universal. We all have responsibilities we cannot avoid. Recognizing your lack of time and then making the necessary changes, however, can be a difficult task. If you recognize you have a problem, begin to make changes as soon as possible—otherwise, things just get worse.

 **It is easy to determine when other people need to make time-management changes, but it can be difficult to recognize the need in yourself. Remember the telltale signs in other people's lives and take a hard look to see if they exist in your life.**

 Conscience is the perfect interpreter of life.

Karl Barth

The Chaos Begins

Hard work is good for the mind, good for the body, and good for the soul. There can come a time, however, when hard work turns into overworked, and busy turns into out of control. The change can be dramatic, but it is often so gradual we don't even notice when or why it happened.

Who, then, is free? The wise man who can govern himself.

Horace

Work with Brenda seemed to change. She was running more than ever and it was common to hear people say, "You do so much," "You never sit down," "I don't know where you get your energy"—and, in truth, Brenda didn't know either. She was always frantically completing "must-do" tasks with deadlines looming over her head.

She wrote list after list. She ran to get work done and to check each task off (and each task seemed to be a project in itself), but her lists continued to grow. Indeed, Brenda felt she was doing so much, but never accomplishing everything.

Things quickly progressed to a point where Brenda's stomach was constantly in knots and she couldn't sleep. Caffeinated drinks were a necessity and sugary snacks became more appealing. The thought of taking time to cook was overwhelming, and fast food and take-out became the meals of choice. To add to the stress, people would comment, "Why aren't you cooking meals? You're a stay-at-home mom!"

Somewhere, despite all her good intentions, it happened: Brenda had totally lost sight of what was important and she was no longer having fun. The chaos was taking over.

Activities and tasks often add up slowly, making it hard to recognize when your life turned into a time-management disaster. An extra few projects at work, a few more responsibilities, just one more addition to what's required in your job description can make for the eventual question, "How'd things get so out of control?" Many people like to be busy and have things to do, but it is often hard to recognize when busy turns into overwhelming and the tasks and activities become all-consuming.

The transition from being busy to being overwhelmed can sneak up on you. If you are already busy, seriously think about how taking on another task will affect your life.

Sudden changes in roles or an addition of jobs can give us more work than we bargained for and can push us into a time crisis. A new job with more pressure and responsibility, a volunteer position involving more than initially met the eye, assuming responsibility for an ill or aging relative, leaving paid employment to stay at home with your children—all these dramatic life changes may require you to make some significant time-management decisions.

When beginning any new job or assuming a new role, the work load is usually initially more than when you become comfortable with the tasks and job duties. Expect an adjustment period with any major life change. The key is to determine whether it will remain too much to handle.

Symptoms of Chaos

Time-management chaos can take our lives by storm, but more commonly it enters gradually. Little by little we take on more, have time for less, and begin to feel . . . *different* about everything we do. Sometimes we don't recognize these signs, but more often we ignore them. Eventually, however, the signs of chaos become so blatant we can't help but see them and recognize that our life is getting out of control.

What are these signs?

People tell you you are taking on too much.

Well-meaning family and friends are usually the first to recognize the chaos creeping into your life but, unfortunately, it's easy to ignore their concerns. They point out aspects of your life you would rather ignore, and you slough it off with "They're overreacting."

It is often family and friends we love the most whom we listen to the least.

Unfortunately, it's all about timing. Until you're ready to hear it, it won't matter how many times the people you love point out your need for change.

Your work space is disorganized.

When you begin to notice stacks of books and papers lying everywhere and discover you're saying "It's here somewhere" more often, you've identified another sign of chaos. No, you don't have to be organized every minute of the day—in fact, many people work well with a few piles and a bit of clutter—but when you can't file one paper because you need to do something with all of them, it's time to take a look at your self-management.

In a minute and **later** are key words in your vocabulary, and you rarely follow up.

When you have the time and people make a request of you, you do the task. A subtle sign of chaos looming in your life is when people ask you to do something, you respond with "later" and never to get back to them. You mean to get back to them but simply never find the time.

Postponing phrases are a busy person's way of saying "I would like to do things for or with you, but I just haven't got the time." Using them too often tells people (correctly or incorrectly) that they are not important enough for you to deal with. Is this the message you want to send?

All changes require transition time. Don't expect to see results overnight. If the changes are positive you'll notice them.

You have trouble sleeping.

Many people in need of time-management overhauls experience difficulty sleeping.

Why?

- *Too many thoughts and ideas are running through your head.* Find time to wind down before bed and learn to turn work off. Lying in bed thinking of tasks to be done takes up valuable sleep time.

- *You're overtired.* Ever had a night you thought for sure you would be asleep the minute your head hit the pillow, only to lie awake for hours? This is the catch-22 of sleeping; if you're too tired, you can't sleep. Sleep when you need to, not only when it's impossible to stay awake.

- *You've had too much caffeine.* With the popularity of coffee and espresso bars, cutting back on caffeine definitely goes against the trend. However, caffeine is a drug that can cause significant problems, especially with sleep. Ironically, we often use caffeine when we're overtired!

Using caffeine can cause a problem that keeps feeding itself. You drink caffeine to stay awake during the day, but it also keeps you awake at night. As a result, you are even more tired the next morning, and you need more caffeine. The more you drink, the worse it gets—you get the idea.

Keeping you awake is all caffeine does. It does not make you as alert, active, productive, and effective as you would be if you had adequate sleep. Cut back on coffee, tea, Coke, Pepsi, chocolate, and other products containing caffeine, and you will have more restful nights. Remember, the cure for lack of sleep is sleep, not artificial stimulants.

- *You've been going to bed too late.* Simple to remedy, but will you? Many people use time in the evening to get the last-minute and the "I just can't do them when people are around" tasks done. Seemingly this is a productive time, but it is often at the expense of much-needed sleep.

  Going to bed will improve your productivity during the day which, in turn, reduces the amount of evening work required.

If you are having trouble sleeping, make a sincere effort to figure out why—then make the necessary changes. More sleep will make you more aware, more productive, and more pleasant to be around!

Set a reasonable bedtime and stick to it. Give yourself the gift of sleep.

You have difficulty sitting.

It's not that your legs won't bend or it hurts your butt to sit on it, but sitting idle is not something you can do. You have too many things to do and too much work to be done to take time to sit and put your feet up. Every minute of the day is filled with activity and, while it would be nice, there is no time to sit.

If you never have time to sit and smell the roses, there is definitely chaos in your life. It's time to re-evaluate.

It is in his pleasure that a man really lives; it is from his leisure that he constructs the true fabric of self.

Agnes Repplier

You have no time for hobbies.

If work has become your hobby and nothing you do is optional, then you have trouble in your life.

Work includes paid employment, raising children, volunteer responsibilities, committee duties, fund-raising activities, household activities, etc.

If you have convinced yourself that sitting to fold laundry or painting the fence is relaxing, you have lost touch with what leisure is. Hobbies are activities you do for yourself, for the fun of it. They are not simply the least stressful items on your list.

Hobbies are essential to a person's well-being. They allow you to escape and become involved in something that is totally recreational, totally for the leisure of it. Relaxation rejuvenates and motivates and is necessary for your well-being. Make time for hobbies.

If you resent others because they don't seem to be working as hard as you are, this may not be a cue for them to get with your pace, but for you to get with theirs.

You experience frequent illnesses.

Getting sick is your body's way of telling you it's time to slow down. Your body requires rest and relaxation to function properly, and when you don't provide these things, it reacts. You may get sick easier, more frequently, and/or more severely. Frequent colds, infections, headaches, susceptibility to seasonal viruses, and the onset of disease can all result when your body doesn't have the energy it needs. Give yourself the gift of health. Slow down.

You have no time for family and friends.

There are times in everyone's life when you put important people on the back burner for a while. You may miss a few special occasions or a dinner with the family or not see a special friend for a while.

It is a problem when you leave these people out for too long and never make them a priority. You can only put off those important people for so long before they begin to feel they are no longer important. You'll discover friends drift away, you receive fewer invitations to casual get-togethers, and family begins to describe you with the preamble "We don't see her much lately, but . . ." Again, it's time to re-evaluate.

People before things.

La Leche League International

Recognize this sign and remedy it as fast as you can. People are what make life, not work.

"Putting out fires" is a normal, everyday activity.

Certainly emergencies arise and become temporary priorities. However, when emergencies become commonplace and every day brings another crisis to be resolved, then chaos exists.

Deadlines exist to help people plan their work and organize their time to fit in required activities. When you become so overburdened with activities that deadlines are no longer a guide but an ax, this is a definite sign that there is too much work on your plate. If all you seem to be doing is putting out fires and scrambling to meet deadlines, managing your time differently is necessary. Do some brainstorming at work to develop some long-term plans or training to rid your day of constant fires.

You have a lack of exercise and a poor diet.

Physical exercise and healthy eating are fundamental elements of maintaining a healthy and productive body. A vehicle runs better when it is regularly maintained and tuned. However, if a vehicle's maintenance is not kept up, its performance decreases. The same is true for your body.

By providing regular exercise and healthy food you increase body performance. You will be healthier, have more energy, and feel better all around. Making time for exercise and eating a well-balanced, nutritious diet are two of the best things you can do for your well-being.

Those who do not find time for exercise will have to find time for illness.

Old Proverb

Reading for fun is a thing of the past.

Reading is one of the great gifts of our era. We can escape to far-off places and imaginary worlds, or we can learn extraordinary amounts.

How does this relate to time management? Well, people who have become overburdened with work often sacrifice the luxury of reading for the sake of enjoyment. Look at what you are reading now compared to what you used to read and decide if your chaos has caused you to forget about this gift.

Stress symptoms appear.

A sure sign of chaos in your life is when stress symptoms are noticeable. Do you have frequent headaches, feel tense in your shoulders, have knots in your stomach, feel anxious, have a heaviness in your chest, and/or get angry easily at those around you? These are some of the symptoms of stress and signals that it's time for change in your life.

Many excellent books on stress and its symptoms have been written. Browse your local library or bookstore for these books.

People need responsibility. They resist assuming it, but they cannot get along without it.

John Steinbeck

The Gift of Chaos

It is easy to think poor time management is your own problem and that others should keep their concerns to themselves, but, in reality, poor time management affects more people than just you.

When Brenda entered a room, others felt the wave of her presence. They felt the need to work a little faster, do a little more, run. At first, this was okay. People were inspired to do more, create more, and be more productive, and Brenda was a motivating role model.

But over time, motivation became anxiety. When Brenda spoke with people about a project, they felt there was a rush, an urgency to the task, and no time to waste, and things had to be done right away. Instead of two weeks' notice, Brenda gave two days' notice, and when she said something had to be done, it had to be done now!

At the end of the day, the work done wasn't always productive. Others felt the tension and confusion Brenda generated, and it was contagious. With less time available, she often did things without thinking, resulting in poor decisions and work that had to be redone. More errors were made and there was "fixing up" after she left. Indeed, those helping Brenda were beginning to dread her calling them. She was creating chaos in her own life and the lives of those she worked with.

Running around looking busy is not productive; it only leaves a wake of anxiety and chaos.

Your time-management problem *is* other people's problem. Chaos is contagious. Therefore, for your sake and for the sake of others, take a look at how you manage yourself in the time you have.

Don't overlook the negative impact you may have on those you work with. These people are your allies; don't alienate them.

You are dumping too much work on others.

You may have begun to help yourself by delegating and recruiting (or forcing) others to help you. This is an excellent way to reduce your work load if done effectively, but if done ineffectively it can actually increase the amount of work you have to do and make the work load on others unmanageable.

Just because you have chosen (yes, chosen) a lifestyle that is a time-management nightmare, this doesn't give you the right to impose it on others. Be considerate of the needs of others.

Be on the lookout for:

- resentment-filled remarks

- signs of weariness

- increased tension when you're around

- people avoiding you

- a decrease in coworker productivity

Take an honest look at how much work you require others to do. Delegating should help you and help others expand their work experience. It should not be a way of dumping unreasonable work onto others so you can breathe more easily.

Cleanup is required when you leave.

If you have become so overworked that you no longer make good decisions, then there will be times when fixing up after you is necessary. If you are aware this is happening, take responsibility for the chaos you are creating and stop it.

People avoid you.

Whether people avoid you because they don't want projects dumped on them or because they don't like the anxiety you leave in your wake, it's evidence you are creating chaos in their lives. Take heed of the warning.

What you do not want done to yourself, do not do to others.

Confucius

Brenda was tired. She had no energy, and her ability to cope was severely diminished. All she wanted to do was get her work done and go to bed.

She still had her family. Like the other areas of her life, she had great intentions of giving them her all, but all she could afford was the bare minimum. "Soon, dear," "I just don't have time," "Just watch one more video"—this was how Brenda was parenting. Her children were fighting more, Brenda's patience was thin, and she spent more time arguing with them than ever. When Dad was home, the children preferred time with him, and the looks of anger directed at Brenda were devastating.

Brenda's husband was a victim as well—a victim of loneliness. When he wasn't working, he was parenting. Because Brenda had so much to do, his hobbies became nonexistent and he had no time for himself. A once-positive relationship became strained with talk of only Brenda's projects. Their love life wasn't exempt; there didn't seem to be time or energy.

Brenda was no longer simply a woman experiencing chaos; she was creating a family experiencing chaos.

You influence those around you, especially those you love most. When you're living in chaos, so are those around you. This reason, and this reason alone, should make you re-evaluate your time and the way you use it.

If you have no one important in your life whom you care if you impact negatively, perhaps your time-management concerns have already pushed people away. This does not give you an out to forget about time management. It should be a hard poke into reality that you need to make changes now!

If you are not spending as much time as you would like with those you say are important to you or if your relationships are not as healthy as they once were, make changes today, before it's too late.

The man who removes a mountain begins by carrying away small stones.

Chinese Proverb

Are you creating chaos in your life? Others may be able to help you answer that question, but only you can make the choice to change.

Top Ten Indicators You Are Experiencing a Time-Management Meltdown

1. You haven't had time to get a haircut and you look like a flower child from the sixties.

2. The supermarket has started ordering more coffee to keep up with your increasing demand.

3. Your coworker's lunch of leftover stew looks like a gourmet meal compared to the take-out you are used to.

4. You fell asleep while being introduced at the engagement where you were to speak.

5. You're thrilled if you're only an hour late for appointments.

6. You put off shopping for clothes too long. Now you're stuck in the washroom because you just blew a zipper.

7. The last time you saw your kids they were twelve. You just received the invitation to their graduation in the mail!

8. You dodged your secretary by slouching behind the stack of papers on your desk.

9. You read last week's memo today and discovered you missed yesterday's luncheon with your boss.

10. You think *Sunday drive* means you can cruise into work faster than any other day of the week.

Chapter 3

The Meaning of Life

Character is what you are in the dark.

Dwight L. Moody

The meaning of life—rather a bold way to open a chapter in any book! Sadly, the answer to the question of why we are on this planet at this particular juncture in time is best answered not in one impact-filled statement but rather by a series of small questions and very, very personal answers.

Life, like time, can be somewhat overwhelming when viewed in its entirety. It helps considerably to break it down a bit into particular moments in your life that helped you become the person you are today—good and bad. Let's call them *defining moments*.

Throughout your life you have experienced, and will continue to experience, many defining moments. In each of them you, and only you, decide how that moment shall unfold. Each moment gives you the opportunity to shape your life as you see fit: to grow, to learn, to teach, and to impact those around you—again, positively or negatively.

I am large, I contain multitudes.

Walt Whitman

Character, also, has everything to do with identifying the meaning of life for any one individual, and defining moments are the building blocks of character. When Robert Frost spoke of taking the path less traveled through the woods, he spoke of a defining moment—a moment when he chose the kind of person he wanted to be. Indeed, he was fully aware of his choices; he chose the road less traveled, and that, in his words, made all the difference.

In work, play, personal relationships, professional relationships, casual meetings, and life-changing encounters, you have the power to decide which path you will choose and how that choice will affect your life and the lives of those around you. You make choices, some positive, some negative, that shape you as an individual—your character, your strength. From that basis you make decisions about time.

Based on the person I am and the person I want to become, what are the important things to put into my day?

Take a sample week of your life and evaluate your activity. Does where you spend your time reflect what is truly important to you? What changes can you make?

efining Moments

What, exactly, is a defining moment?

A defining moment is a specific moment in your life when you have the opportunity to change the course of your life. Now, don't get frightened, overwhelmed, or panicky here! Sometimes these moments come in the simplest forms, in seemingly meaningless situations. These smallest of moments, however, often have the largest of ripples.

Your son has been talking about quitting school. He claims there is nothing there for him to learn to help him with the business of living. You don't particularly care what he thinks he can and can't learn by going straight to work; you want him to graduate. You've already had a couple of heated arguments, and the situation is at a standstill. You nag and lecture, and he persists and ignores.

It's very early on a Sunday morning and you find yourself in the quiet of the kitchen, finishing a presentation for work, when your son comes home from bartending at a local nightclub. You've made coffee, and he hops up on the counter to sit and have a cup with you. He's tired and feeling low-key, and he opens a conversation about school.

For a brief second you feel that familiar defensive anxiety in the pit of your stomach as you prepare to enter into battle. You take a breath and open your mouth to launch into full lecture mode, . . . and then, in one of those moments of genuine clarity, you close it and your son begins to speak.

You have just had a defining moment, and in that moment you decided it was time to take a new approach. It was time to trust that the man sitting hunched over on the counter, your son, had some important and valid things to say. You decided to choose a new path, to listen. You had a defining moment, one that may have changed forever your relationship with your son.

Although you have probably experienced far more defining moments than you can immediately remember, take a moment to try and recall moments when you felt your life direction took a turn. How did you feel, what did you do, and what would you change?

The significant problems we face cannot be solved by the same level of thinking that created them.

Albert Einstein

How do we know a moment is a defining one?

A moment when you need to look deep within yourself and question what is sincerely important to you now and for the future, that is a defining moment.

There are those defining moments in life, we've all had them, when things tend to move in slow motion.

For of all sad words of tongue
    or pen,
The saddest are these: "It might
    have been."

John Greenleaf Whittier

Consider:

You are scheduled to have an important meeting with your boss. You don't know what the meeting is about prior to it, only that she wants to see you. It starts out well, with talk of how nicely you have progressed with the company—that you're a natural leader and a quick learner and have a real knack for the industry. Somewhere along the way the tone of the conversation changes, however, and you quickly realize you are being asked to significantly change your life. In order for you to succeed, to reach your maximum capacity with the company (to progress, is what you hear), you will need to spend considerably more time at the office.

In that brief second, time stands still. You think of your new baby at home. You think of the personal and professional gains you have received working with this organization. You think about the things you do and don't like about your work. You think about the increase in pay that would come with the increase in responsibility. You think of all these things in that slow-motion split second when you realize you are being asked to make a life decision.

40

You consider the person you are and the person you are striving to become. You consider the people around you, at home and at the office, and what you are to them. You wonder in that fraction of an instant if you have what it takes to make this decision. Then somewhere, deep in the pit of your stomach, you feel what the right answer is, the right answer for you.

You have just had a defining moment—a brief moment in time when you had the potential to change the course of your life. Often these moments feel as if some outside force is acting upon us, slowing things down, hoping we'll reflect on our actions and assign them the importance they deserve.

We promise according to our hopes, and perform according to our fears.

François La Rochefoucauld

Ultimately you know you have had a defining moment by the intensity of your feeling afterward. If you have followed your instincts and reflected on your principles and your values, a defining moment will make you feel powerful and clear, fully aware of the impact potential of the time, and stronger when the moment is over.

For example:

- You have said no to taking on additional volunteer work because it would take too much valuable time away from your family.

- You have declined a job transfer because in the long run it wouldn't fit with your personal mission statement (see page 50).

- You have taken a long look at your behavior with your spouse, realized it was seriously jeopardizing the relationship, and gone about redefining old habits and patterns.

Any and all of these are defining moments. You paused for thought, considered how much time you had to give and what was *genuinely* important, and you made a decision. It may have meant saying no to people who were important to you, missing out on money from a career move, or having to admit you didn't particularly like the person you currently were, all of which define you, your values, and your character, making those decisions easier next time.

Gavin was in a well-paying but high-stress, time-consuming career, and he wasn't even sure he liked it. He had difficulty making any decisions because he no longer knew what was important to him. He discussed it with his wife and after much soul-searching they both took leave from work to travel and rediscover what was important—something they always said they would do.

Continuous effort—not strength or intelligence—is the key to unlocking our potential.

Liane Cordes

If, however, in a defining moment you go against your better judgment, succumbing to peer pressure, greed, vanity, or your ego, you will often feel anxious and weak, wishing desperately you could have the moment back to do again.

How do we make the moment count? With work, personal growth, maturity, wisdom, soul-searching, integrity, honesty, accountability. Only *you* can guide your defining moments. Only you can determine which direction you need to go. Only you can hear that little voice inside you pushing you in the right direction.

It's no use crying over spilt milk: it only makes it salty for the cat.

Anonymous

What does this have to do with time management?

Defining moments, character, and what you deem important in your life have everything to do with time management. Defining moments build and create character. Character defines who you are and what is important to you and your life. Knowing what is important to you and how it will affect your life and its direction is precisely what time management is about.

We have already come to terms with the fact that we cannot manage time, we can only manage ourselves. Therefore, knowing exactly what is important and meaningful to you, your life, and your growth makes it markedly easier to decide where to spend your time.

The Chicken or the Egg?

The age-old question: which came first, the chicken or the egg? Is there an answer?

Well, yes.

It's all about perspective. Each of us as an individual has a certain set of values, ideals, and belief systems which slant our perspective on all things we experience in life. For example, if you have deep-seated religious values, believing God created the universe and all in it, you would probably suggest God created the chicken and the chicken laid the first egg. If, on the other hand, you are a scientist to the core and an atheist, chances are you would have a scientific notion about molecules of hydrogen, single-celled organisms, evolution, and the resulting chicken embryo. You may be a strict vegetarian and have ignored the entire question for years. Whatever your answer may be, it's all based on perspective.

Similarly, we speak of defining moments, character, and time management in that particular order. However, once again, it's all about perspective. Each of us has had many defining moments throughout our lives. Some of them we are aware of, some we are not. These moments help define our character, which, in turn, enables us to set time priorities.

The only way of discovering
the limits of the possible is to
venture a little way past them into
the impossible.

Arthur C. Clarke

Now, change the perspective, and it is our character that allows us to triumph in various defining moments. Based on the type of person we are and aspire to be, we make choices that direct and mold our life accordingly. We thus manage ourselves in the time we have, accordingly.

Back to the chicken and the egg. It is obvious one had to come first. We will concede, however, that which one did is still up for continued debate. On which comes first, defining moments or well-developed character, the answer is—you can't actually have one without the other. Every defining moment is a test of character, and you must have a sense of who you are (character) to navigate a defining moment.

Think of a defining moment in your life. Did you grow because of it? Were you strong in your focus before, simply finding that the moment redefined your position? Or both?

The point? This is the essence of effective time management. Time management is life management. The meaning of life is what you make of it. Who do you want to be, what kind of person do you want to be—how do you want to affect others: your family, friends, lovers? We only have a finite time here, and because of that, it is important to decide early on what is important to you. Indeed, it is a tall order to ask people if they really know themselves, if they really know what it is that is important, and if they really know what it is that makes them passionate.

Start now to decide what in your life cannot wait until tomorrow. Forget about the past; you only waste more precious time and energy worrying about what you should, could, or would have done. Begin today with what you perpetually ignore. Stop saying over and over to yourself, "Tomorrow, tomorrow I will give those projects or people the attention they deserve."

 Not heaven itself upon the past
has power.

John Dryden

How?

In theory it all sounds so easy. You simply decide what is not important to you, stop doing it, and then use all this extra time to do the things that are close to your heart. Well, sort of. Let's take a look at it from another perspective.

Selfish or Focused?

Two of the most prominent lessons we learn and can probably remember from childhood are:

1. Don't brag too much about yourself or your accomplishments.

2. You must learn to share.

Somewhere in the learning of those lessons or the confusion of the terminology, we ended up as adults thinking:

1. What you need isn't really that important.

2. If someone asks nicely for something, never say no.

Unfortunately, many of us have taken the modified lessons and made an art form of their practice, putting our own needs on hold and taking on added responsibilities because saying no makes us feel guilty. This is a major contributor to our time deficit. So why do we continue to do it? Because we got confused with the rules and think if we don't continue on with it people will think we are selfish.

All things are difficult before they are easy.

Thomas Fuller

Let's clear this up once and for all.

Knowing what you want, being passionate about what you want and being focused in your work toward what you want, does *not* make you selfish. Selfishness happens when you expect everyone to abandon what is important to them to aid you in the sole pursuit of your interests.

Much of the confusion occurs when you begin to say no to people who ask you to distract yourself from your goals to assist them in some way. You do not have to be involved in everything everyone in your life is doing, and it would be false of you to pretend to be. If those people are important to you, being interested in them as individuals and how their life activities make them feel is what matters.

Once you un-learn, or at least relearn, the definition of selfish, it should be much easier to decide if you fit within that definition. It is not, repeat *not selfish* to say no to people who are asking you to commit your time to a project you do not feel strongly about. As a matter of fact, you would do well to say no and let them accept that.

Are you selfish? What in your life do you do only for you? Do you expect others to drop everything to participate in this activity? Now, again, are you selfish?

If you are not strongly committed to something, it is difficult to dedicate time to doing it well. Add to that the feeling that you were pressured into something you did not have time for in the first place and not only will you not give it the attention it deserves, it won't be long before you begin to resent the entire thing and the person who got you involved.

We cannot do everything. We have established that, and trying to do it all is killing us. We have no time for ourselves, we have no time for the people we say are important to us, and we are experiencing so much stress in our lives we aren't able to do anything really well.

It is also not selfish, repeat *not selfish* to take time in your life for you. To do what you enjoy alone, or with people you enjoy spending time with, is not selfish; it is essential. If you are not happy, you are not healthy, and if you are not healthy you are not able to keep any of the time commitments you have made. Take time for yourself.

To love oneself is the beginning of a life-long romance.

Oscar Wilde

Once again, what does all this have to do with time management? Time management is about realizing boundaries. It's about foresight. It's about letting go of past behavior and having the courage to grow. It's about defining who you are and where you want to spend your time and not feeling guilty for it. Over and over it's been said that you cannot manage time, you can only manage yourself, and self-management begins with knowing what's important to you and establishing parameters around that.

It's important to clearly understand the difference between what it means to be selfish and what it means to be focused. Why? Because if you feel you are being selfish it is considerably easier to be swayed from a decision.

Consider an important decision you've made. On what did you base your decision? Were you pressured to change your mind? Did you? Why or why not?

For example, you have agreed to coordinate the second grade Christmas play. You realize it is a huge commitment, but you've thought about it and it's something you always wanted to do, you have some great ideas to make it fun for the kids, and your daughter is in the play. Now, volunteers are at a premium this year and the school is having trouble finding someone to assist with the choral segment of the production. Someone suggested you might be a good person to do it since you're already involved, your daughter is in the production and you're there for rehearsals, you have great ideas for the play and for the music, and it would only be an additional hour or two per week. The pressure is on.

What do you do? Every argument they have is valid, no one else is volunteering, and the kids really want to sing. Do you agree, yes or no? No.

Why? You spent a lot of time considering your ability to commit fully to the dramatic portion of the Christmas project. You took into account not only rehearsal time with the children, but time you would have to spend calling parents to arrange costuming, schedule rehearsals, coordinate snacks, and recruit additional volunteers to assist with supervision and transportation when necessary. Countless other duties would undoubtedly come up as Christmas and the play drew closer. You knew all of this and decided you could afford the time and do a good job of one major project, not two. This wasn't something you planned to do every year, but you did plan, at least once a year, to participate in a leadership capacity in one of your daughter's major projects, be it a skating party, camping trip, or science fair.

Are you being selfish? No.

 Still as of old, men by themselves
are priced—For thirty pieces Judas
sold himself, not Christ.

Hester H. Cholmondeley

You have established your boundaries. You, of all people, know your limits and how much you can take on in your life effectively. You decided systematically what was important to you (your daughter), what you valued (being positively involved in her life), and how you could make that a part of your life (do the play). Undoubtedly you had to put other things on hold to make time in your life to be the play director, and you no doubt had to flatly say no to other things because they simply were not as important to you. The choral segment of the show is no different. You do not have an unlimited amount of time, and you must choose, guilt free. *Note: this does get easier with practice!*

When you take an objective look at it, this decision is not that complicated. You decided your daughter and her play were a priority and that you would sacrifice what was necessary to do a good job with her and with the play. Now you have been asked to take on added responsibilities, which sound harmless enough off the top. You know, however, that as the performance draws near there will be more to do and the time requirements will increase considerably with both the dramatic and choral components of the evening.

Will you do what you set out to do and do it well? Or will you be pressured into taking on an additional role and spread yourself so thin that you'll have difficulty accomplishing your initial goal? Suddenly the decision isn't all that difficult to make.

Are you being selfish? No, you are being realistic and honest.

 **Are there times in your life when you bit off more than you could chew? How would you manage that situation differently now?**

Be honest with yourself. As difficult as it can be at times, be honest with yourself and those around you. Know what is important to you and be realistic about how you can use the time you have available to you. Above all else, be confident you have made informed, realistic, rational, and enlightened choices that are right for you. You have established boundaries, taken responsibility for your time, and planned for the future; now stick to your guns! Do not become a dumping ground for projects other people are unwilling to take on.

 A successful person is one who can lay a firm foundation with the bricks that others throw at him or her.

David Brinkley

Your Mission

A company's mission statement is its public statement to employees and clients of what is important to that particular organization. It defines in concise, easy-to-understand language what a company believes in, strives to accomplish, and plans for the future.

A mission statement is unique to every organization in its language and format but universal in that it is the fundamental objective and underlying motive for that which the company does. If it is well incorporated into the organization it is truly a guiding principle for decision making, goal setting, and management of daily operations.

 LB

Dana was changing careers and, after many sacrifices, she was going back to school. At the beginning of the year she found herself pressured into working for her old boss on a project he said no one else could complete. Not long after beginning, Dana found herself behind in her schoolwork, angry for agreeing to take on the project, and resentful of her old boss for pressuring her into it. She took the time to re-evaluate, realized the work was no longer important to her personal mission, and informed her old boss she would no longer work on the project.

A personal mission statement is no different. It is unique in its language and format, but universal in its function. Interestingly enough, it is often more challenging to compose a personal mission statement than it is to outline one for a multinational organization.

Why?

Very few of us have ever bothered to take the time to sincerely think about what it is we want in life. More often than not, we fumble through life randomly making decisions and accepting or declining opportunity as it comes to us rather than having a plan and a direction.

This is not to suggest your life has been a waste of time till now! Everything you do in life is about learning and growing, which, hopefully, you have done.

A mission statement is not, however, just about goal setting. Goals are certainly part of the statement, but they are not all of it. Your mission statement defines:

- who you are

- what you value

- what kind of person you want to be

- what is important to you

- what impact you want to have on those around you

What does this have to do with time management? Everything.
Your mission statement is about who you are as a person. It is about what you want to make of yourself and the world around you. It outlines your beliefs, your desires, your needs, and your hopes. When you have truly completed a mission statement for yourself, honestly considered what it represents, and continually worked to integrate it into your daily life, it will become the foundation from which you manage your life.

That which we persist in doing becomes easier—not that the nature of the task has changed, but our ability to do has increased.

Ralph Waldo Emerson

Over and over again we have stressed how you can only manage yourself, not time, and you can only manage yourself according to what is important to you. If you do not fully understand, accept, and take responsibility for what is important to you, you are fumbling around making decisions with no guidelines within which to make them.

It is not uncommon to become so caught up in the activity of doing things, the sheer business of living, that you suddenly wake up one morning and realize you are not at all going in the direction you thought.

A mission statement is a guide, the standard by which all things are judged: your center, your ground, your lifeline, your prime directive. Whatever you choose to label it, it is one thing: essential to self-management. When you know from where you come, what is important to you and for you, the choice of what you spend your time on becomes inconceivably easier.

Again, this is not to suggest that your life up to this point, without a personal mission statement, has been a complete waste of time. That would be ridiculous. What it does suggest, however, is you may have been taking on too much and feeling guilty about leaving things incomplete or haphazardly accomplished because you have not been able to say no to projects and tasks coming your way.

Many of us are guilty of basing our life decisions on what others believe is good for us. We often listen to everyone but ourselves when it comes to making important decisions, trying to please the people close to us. We participate in herd mentality (following mindlessly along as one of the group), not wanting to rock the boat, break any rules, or ruffle any feathers, thinking we are safe when all we are is numb.

We must not cease from exploration. And the end of all our exploring will be to arrive where we began and to know the place for the first time.

T. S. Eliot

With no core, center, or foundation to use to judge if projects are worth your time and attention, it is easy to see how time management becomes random, hit-and-miss. It is difficult for you to say no to things because you may feel you have no real reason to say no, no burning passion to spend your time elsewhere. With a personal mission statement that you have spent some quality time developing (and it will evolve), comes an inner strength of purpose. Something you may have once taken on out of a feeling of guilt or obligation, you can now objectively evaluate based on whether or not it:

- fits with your objectives

- will help you or someone you love grow as a person

- takes time away from something more important to you

- will enhance your quality of life in the future (for example, taking time you may not feel you have to train employees to fill a broader role at the office)

 **Consider how you have made decisions in the past. What priorities did you use? Were you consistently happy with your decisions?**

How do you go about writing this master plan? First you must set aside the time to do it! Take some time alone, on a day you will not be interrupted, and clear your mind of all other things. Forget, if only for a couple of hours, the projects at work sitting on your desk, your kids' baseball game you promised to umpire tomorrow, and all other busy thoughts which dominate your brain.
Consider:

1. Each of us plays many different roles in a lifetime. You may be: parent, spouse, employer, community advocate, church member, child, and so on. With each of these roles come responsibilities and expectations. Your mission statement, as you write it, needs to reflect the impact you want to have in each of these roles—who am I to these people, and who do I want to be, now and in the future?

2. You are responsible for your life, for everything you do, only you. You cannot blame anyone but yourself for your lack of time. Try as you might to say "My spouse expects me to," "I have to do this and that for my kids," "If I don't do this for my boss," ultimately it is you who takes on that stuff. You are an individual with the freedom to choose where you spend your time. Perhaps you are just out of practice with the choice part!

3. Your mission statement is about aligning your behavior with your beliefs. It is about asking yourself if you are driven by outside circumstances, things that happen to you, or are you guided from within by your belief in yourself and your desires for yourself?

Frankly, are you walking the walk or simply talking the talk? It is one thing to write what is important to you and what you believe in, where you want to go and how you want to get there, but to live it on a daily basis takes devotion, discipline, and persistence until you genuinely integrate your mission statement into your life.

There are cultures on the planet not as obsessed with time as we in the West are. In fact, some cultures do not even calculate age chronologically by year. The individual chooses the time to mark personal growth, development of character, or entrance into a new stage of life with a celebration. Members of the community gather to honor that individual and his or her accomplishments, not simply the passage of time.

Expect that your mission statement will evolve as you age, as you experience more, and as you become clearer about what moves you. Indeed, after you have written yours, it may take several rewrites over several weeks or months till it feels as though it fits. Do not despair; you may, in fact, find the writing of your mission statement as valuable as having the final product.

When All Is Said and Done

The meaning of life is truly the age-old question, one which has intrigued human beings perhaps for all time. Ultimately, when all is said and done we must be happy with ourselves; we must be happy with what we have accomplished, with how we have touched the lives of those around us—those we know and love and those whose paths we may have only briefly crossed.

Perhaps that is one way to approach life—by considering the end first. When you are gone and the people close to you reflect on your life and the kind of person you were, what most do you want them to say, to remember? Carefully consider that as you compose your personal mission statement.

The fountain of content must spring up in the mind, and he who hath so little knowledge of human nature as to seek happiness by changing anything but his own disposition, will waste his life in fruitless efforts and multiply the grief he proposes to remove.

Samuel Johnson

We touch other people's lives while we are on the planet. What kind of impact do you want to have? Your character and fundamental nature are tested daily as people demand more of you, more of your time. What will you do? In those defining moments, will you know what is important and stick to your guns, or will you succumb to pressure and add more to your exponentially expanding in-basket? Remember, your life, your path, your choice.

An Afterthought

Perhaps the meaning of life is infinitely more simple than we believe. Perhaps to smile a genuine smile and to touch another with that feeling each day—maybe that is the true meaning of life.

Managing Yourself

For every thousand hacking at the
leaves of evil, there is one striking at
the root.

Henry David Thoreau

So, you've defined your values and created your personal mission statement. Great, you've got it all, time management done! Now everything will just fall into place. Right?

Wrong!

If that's all there was to time management we wouldn't have so many people with time trouble in our society. We frequently hear the value statements: "My family comes first," "I live for time away from work," but people's actions are often inconsistent with these values: "The twenty hours of overtime I put in this month will really help pay for our new car," "I know I said I'd play ball with you, but I have too many other things to get done." Living our lives so they reflect our values is where the true challenge lies.

Like an ability or muscle, hearing
your inner wisdom is strengthened
by doing it.

Robbie Gass

Taking Responsibility

What does responsibility have to do with time management? You're probably a responsible person who can meet the most restrictive deadline, you've never missed a car payment, so why do you need to talk about taking responsibility? Well, frankly, that's the easy stuff. Being responsible to *yourself* is a little different.

What?

How you spend your time is not an accident, is not left to fate, and is not out of your control. The decisions and choices you make determine how manageable your time and life is.

Try to keep your soul young and quivering right up to old age, and to imagine right up to the brink of death that life is only beginning. I think that is the only way to keep adding to one's talent, to one's affections, and one's inner happiness.

George Sand

Bea and Donald were aspiring accountants, but their grades were not good enough to get them into university. Bea was devastated when she was rejected from university and went to work as cashier at a local grocery store.

Donald was unhappy as well, but he realized that all avenues were not closed. He applied to a community college for a two-year accounting program and was accepted. After completing the program, he worked as an accountant and did extremely well. A year and a half later he decided he still wanted to be a certified accountant and applied again to university. In his application, he included his grades from college and his performance reports from work and described his great desire to be a certified accountant. Within a few months Donald was accepted to university and is now a certified accountant.

Bea continues her job as a cashier but has never really been happy with her job. She blames it on her marks, saying there was nothing she could do.

Taking responsibility for your own choices is a huge step in life. It is up to you to realize that your actions and decisions affect where you go, the things that happen to you, and who you become. Your life is your responsibility.

Your lack of time is also your responsibility. It is not your boss's fault for dumping so much on you, it is not the government's fault there aren't any good jobs, and it's not your kids' faults that they have lots of energy. You decide whether or not to take on the added responsibilities, you stop looking for other work, you take the easy way out with the excuses. The choices (yes, they may be difficult ones) are yours. It's your responsibility to choose how you will manage your time.

Do you make choices based on what you say is important? Once you begin to do this, you are truly beginning to take responsibility for your time.

Responsibility Paralyzers

Time management is a decision-making activity, and here's where the excuses begin! Without even thinking about it, we easily make excuses for our lack of time management, for *why* we can't (or don't) make the necessary choices and changes in our lives. Flippant remarks and excuses in our heads paralyze us from managing ourselves and making the changes necessary to get our lives under control.

The more a person is able to direct his life consciously, the more he can use time for constructive benefits.

Rollo May

Which of these sound familiar?

- *There isn't enough time in my day* . . . If you find yourself wishing for a thirty-hour day, stop. It won't happen. Even if it did, eventually you'd wish for a forty-hour day. The problem is not how long the day is but how much you cram into it. The next time you find yourself wishing for more time in the day, evaluate the long-term importance of the activities you've chosen. Time management is not about fitting thirty hours into twenty-four; it is about streamlining so twenty-four is enough.

- *If I had time I would* . . . */I just don't have time* . . . If this is your excuse for not making time for things that are important (refer to your mission statement), stop using it! If you say you value people or an activity, then prove it. Empty excuses allow you to put important tasks aside and never get back to them.

- *I don't have a choice* . . . You always have a choice, period. Granted, the choice may not be an easy one or the repercussions may be serious, but you always have a choice in every situation.

- *That's just the way it is* . . . Never! There is always room for change, growth, and modification. Even if you have chosen something in the past, it isn't written in stone. You have the power to change anything from the way it is to the way you want it.
    It's your choice.

- *I've always done it that way* . . . Live for today and plan for tomorrow, and many more options and possibilities arise. The past is meant to learned from, not relived.

- *They can't do it without me* . . . This is your ego talking. Everyone is replaceable. When you retire, the company won't fall apart without you. When you quit doing everything for your children, they'll begin doing it for themselves. When you give up playing volleyball, the team will find another player.
    People and activities will go on without you. They may be accomplished more or less efficiently and will most likely be

completed differently than you would have done them, but they will get done.

Your decision to change will affect *you* more positively than it will affect others negatively. Make decisions for yourself, not for others.

- *Everyone else is doing it; I must have to . . .* The illusion of having to keep up can get you into serious time-management difficulties. There is nothing saying you have to do things the way others do, have the same things they do, or accomplish as much. Decide what you want from life and go for it! Forget trying to keep up, and focus on accomplishing what you want.

Quit paralyzing yourself with excuses and rationalizations. Choose to do things that fulfill your goals and expectations and are consistent with your values, and stop doing the rest.

 Very often a change of self is needed more than a change of scene.

A. C. Benson

Sometimes it seems that no matter what you say there are tasks forced upon you. What about these?

- *There are too many tasks in your job description.* Engage in some long-range planning—train those around you to share some responsibility. Evaluate your strengths and the strengths of those you work with, and share duties accordingly.

- *Your boss gives you a must-do project you feel you don't have time for.* Evaluate the importance of the project with respect to your other tasks. In the long term, will completing this task make your life easier? Effective time management plans for the future.

What projects eating up your time are really not important? Are you confusing urgent, in-your-face problems with those that are genuinely important to your day, your life, your future?

For example, which is more important, continuing your meeting with your secretary who is compiling a training manual for staff, or answering the phone? We are often distracted by whatever is loudest—the squeaky wheel. Constantly remind yourself what is important in the long term. Where is your time best spent?

Continue your meeting with your secretary; let voice mail get the phone.

- *You have to drive your child to yet another activity.* Carpool, or next semester don't enroll her in so many things. Cutting back will give you more time and give your child time to do her own things as well.

- *You have too many household responsibilities.* Lower your expectations. You don't have to be able to eat off the floor, your shirts can be worn twice, and the grass can grow more than one centimeter before it needs cutting.

 These options may not be easy but may be realistic in order for you to be true to yourself, and that's what time management is really all about.

Stop allowing others (including your boss, spouse, family, friends, everyone) to manage your time and your life. If you don't like what's happening, say no, or make changes, but forget the "I don't have a choice" excuse; it simply doesn't cut it!

onsiderate Decisions

Manage yourself—manage time. It's all about choices. You've been making choices all along. Now the key is to make good ones!

 We choose our joys and sorrows long before we experience them.

Kahlil Gibran

Choices are not made effortlessly, and it takes patience and practice to become good at making decisions.

Stop Being a Dumping Ground for Other People's Projects

Don't stop helping out when and where you can. Do stop taking over everything that comes your way.

Most of the things we decide are not what we know to be best. We say yes, merely because we are driven into a corner and must say something.

Dr. Frank Crane

Use Your Mission Statement to Help You Make Decisions

If you use this statement and refer to it regularly, it can truly help you get your life in order. But if it is filed and forgotten, the exercise of identifying it will have been a waste of time. Every decision you make should be consistent with the values and mission statement you develop.

Organizations make value decisions every day. La Leche League Canada (LLLC) is a breast-feeding information and support organization with groups across Canada. In 1995 LLLC was approached with a business proposition that would have allowed its pamphlets to be included in packages given to mothers with new babies. Initially this seemed like a great way to provide information to new mothers, but it conflicted with LLLC policy. LLLC does not accept services funded by formula manufacturers (their goals contradict LLLC's goal of helping mothers learn to breast-feed their babies), and the organization that approached LLLC was partially sponsored by formula manufacturers. Therefore, LLLC declined the offer.

LLLC stood by its values and philosophy as an organization. And while it may seem an opportunity was missed, the integrity and commitment of the organization remained in tact, thus opening even more doors for the future.

If each of us had our own personal board of directors to make decisions for us, we might make decisions more consistent with our values. Unfortunately, this is not the case. We must each take responsibility for our choices and decisions.

If, after all, men cannot always make history have a meaning, they can always act so that their own lives have one.

Albert Camus

You can, however, be as personally accountable to your mission statement as companies are to theirs. Granted, it takes thought, effort, and dedication, but it's worth it in the long run.

- Type or neatly write your mission statement and make several copies. Display them at work, at home, on your calendar, and in your weekly planner. Whenever you find yourself faced with a defining moment there will be no question of your personal mission.

- When asked to make a decision that could result in a time commitment, consciously refer to your list and determine if the activity is consistent with one of your value statements.

- If a request fits with your personal mission statement, decide if you have the time to dedicate to the task. Remember, just because your career is a priority doesn't mean you must spend every waking moment working. Work at balancing your life in all directions.

- Decline requests that are inconsistent with your mission statement. Even when a request seems like an opportunity, if it goes against the things you believe in, you would be sacrificing your integrity, and your integrity is the foundation of your character.

- Learn to say no. Some of us have forgotten how to use it guilt free, but *no* shows we have a will and can make decisions. No, when used thoughtfully, is incredibly empowering.

Your mission statement is a powerful tool and key to successful self- and time management. Use it.

Make Long-Term Goals Before Making Short-Term Ones

Long-term goals help you keep things in perspective and are good gauges of whether your behavior today will help you accomplish the things you want in the long run.

 Plan your week before planning your day. This ensures you don't get caught up in the little tasks but keep the larger goals in mind.

Plan for Only Twenty-Four Hours in a Day (with Seven to Ten Hours of Sleep per Night)

There will be tasks that are consistent with your mission statement but you honestly don't have time for. Doing a few things well is infinitely better than doing many things halfway.

 Remember, twenty-four hours in a day!

Don't Try to Manage Every Minute of the Day

Some events simply cannot be planned and managed to the minute. We have all heard the phrase "quality instead of quantity," but, sadly, quality time is often something that cannot be planned, and it certainly cannot be crammed into a specified time slot.

Plan your week to allow enough free time for quality to emerge, evolve, and appear in your life. Don't expect it to happen in the two hours you penciled in and then be disappointed if quality isn't the experience.

 **Slotted time for family and friends can make them feel only as important as your next meeting. If your friendship "meetings" usually end with "I wish I could stay, but . . .," it's time for you to start treating these people with more respect.**

There will always be times when your life becomes a rush or when you are faced with serious time-management decisions. Always refer back to your mission statement and make choices consistent with it. Good decisions will get easier to make, and your time will be better spent.

our Approach

If you are used to the rigid scheduling, planning, and list-making time-management strategies of old, it will take time to get used to this less structured, but more effective, approach to self-management. You will need to get used to identifying your values, planning for the future, and saying no.

Allow yourself to experience setbacks. Few tasks (including trying to do fewer tasks) are ever done perfectly the first time. Give yourself a break, and keep at it.

 Providence has hidden a charm in difficult undertakings which is appreciated only by those who dare to grapple with them.

Madame Swetchine

How?

Make Changes Slowly

Making extreme changes in your life can cause confusion and disorder.

Think of your life as like a pendulum. If the change is too drastic in one direction, the pendulum reaches its limit and swings back the other way. When things get tough, you swing back to the other side.

However, if you make changes slowly, the pendulum simply slows down at a controlled and manageable pace.

Change slowly, but change. Begin by making little changes, changing parts of your life with smaller consequences, then gradually move on to larger and more significant things.

 Only you know how well you can handle changes. Make them at your own pace.

 When you encounter difficulties and contradictions, do not try to break them, but bend them with gentleness and time.

Saint Francis of Sales

Expect and Plan for Setbacks

Don't expect to realign your time-management practices overnight. Expect this to be a slow process with immeasurable reward. Remember, you are dusting off your values and learning to live by them—reeducation is a time-consuming process.

It took some time to implement all this chaos into your life. Expect it to take some time to eliminate it!

 Self-management is a process, not an event. You will have good and bad times, but it is the overall progress that matters.

Control What You Can and Leave the Rest

Some events are out of your control, but how you choose to react to them is within your control. Instead of dwelling on things and events you cannot change, accept that fact and move on to situations where you do have impact. Life is about making the most and best of what you're given.

 **A considerable amount of time is lost when you dwell upon things over which you have no control. Are you a compulsive worrier, a routine "What if"-er, or an obsessed "If I could only change . . ." thinker? If you are, you are wasting valuable time.**

Do the Tasks You Don't Like

There are things in everybody's life they hate doing but must be done. You may need to type memos, give sales presentations, do laundry, or get up with the baby six times in the night, period. You don't have to love doing it, but do it quickly and without procrastinating and complaining.

 One hour of pain completing a task you hate, followed by six hours of pleasure is preferable to agonizing your whole day over the unpleasant task that must be done. If you have unpleasant tasks to do, get them over and done with early.

Enjoy the Things You Do

Plan to treat yourself when you finish a project you didn't like, hum to yourself while waiting in line to pay your bills, or tickle your baby as you change her dirty diaper. No task has to be unbearable, and it is your choice to make it fun. If you make unpleasant tasks fun, imagine how great interesting tasks will be!

Manage Yourself, Not Time

We incorrectly believe if we are more efficient and use our time more effectively our problems will be solved. This is untrue. There is only so much time in a day; there is only so much you can do. Learn to make decisions based on what is important in your life, and eliminate those things that simply use up time.

Maintain a Positive Attitude

Even if things aren't exactly how you want them yet, remember that no matter what happens you choose how you will react. Instead of looking at how bad things are, think how great they'll be when you unlearn some bad habits. Instead of lamenting how much work you have, focus on the fact that you really enjoy what you do. Instead of dwelling on criticism from a customer, dwell on your positive relationship with your partner.

So much of our happiness depends on perspective and attitude. Yes, there will be days when nothing goes your way and the world seems to be against you, and those will be the days to re-evaluate. Remember what is important to you, and make changes again.

Conclusion

It's difficult when you're young, healthy, and vibrant to consider a time when that may not necessarily be so. Indeed, it seems to be part of the human condition to forget that we are, in fact, mortal beings and that there is an eventual end to our time on Earth.

"Good grief," you're thinking, "this is just a time-management book!" True enough, but we don't have an infinite length of time here, so we need, desperately, to make the time we have count. We are a society that forever puts things off to tomorrow: tomorrow I will make time, tomorrow I will change, tomorrow I will make it up to you, tomorrow I will become the person I want to be, tomorrow . . .

There comes a time in your life when tomorrow has to arrive. You picked this book for a reason—a book on time management, a book supporting values, change, and self-management. Maybe tomorrow is finally here.

Took My Time at Twelve

"It skipped seven times
      let's try for eight."
I'd hurry home if
      i knew i was late
Don't look for me
      i'm trading cards
Running with friends
      through strange backyards
Rocks to throw
      doorbells to ring
"you—caan't—catch—mee!"
      i didn't do a thing

Where did it go
      how did it stop?
I think it was the day
      I got my first watch.

Gerry Mattia

✓